The
Believer's
Guide On Personal
Evangelism

———— ✦ ————

A Study Course

DR. JOHN THOMAS WYLIE

authorHOUSE®

AuthorHouse™
1663 Liberty Drive
Bloomington, IN 47403
www.authorhouse.com
Phone: 1 (800) 839-8640

Published by AuthorHouse 05/07/2019

ISBN: 978-1-7283-1117-3 (sc)
ISBN: 978-1-7283-1116-6 (e)

Contents

CHAPTER ONE

CHAPTER TWO

CHAPTER THREE

CHAPTER FOUR

CHAPTER FIVE

CHAPTER SIX

Study Questions

Introduction

The Great Commission
(A Worldwide Commission)

JESUS REPORTED HIS PROGRAM and a crisis hour was struck ever of. The peak is found in His Great Commission: "All power is given unto me in heaven and in earth. Go ye therefore, and teach all nations, baptizing them in the name of the Father, and of the Son, and of the Holy Ghost: Teaching them to observe all things whatsoever I have commanded you: and, lo, I am with you alway, even unto the end of the world (Matthew 28: 18-20 KJV).

On what mission were they sent? To overwhelm, or overrun the world with armed forces (armies) and make men to submit under the sword? No, but to "make disciples of all nations."

From the mountaintop of His ascension His disciples began forth on this mission, radiating from that center, and they have gone on until they everywhere reached the edge of the world. Christianity is no national or racial religion. It knows no limits of mountain or ocean, however it encompasses, it envelopes the globe.

The primary prerequisite made of the disciples of Jesus Christ after the call to follow Him was that they ought to move toward becoming "Fishers of men..." This fresh start of life with their master was to request an adjustment in needs (a change in priorities). Their talents were to be diverted to retrieving people.

The learning procedure or process was identified with their following Him. There is an indistinguishable connection between being in close fellowship with the Lord Jesus Christ and the desire, the longing to bring people to salvation.

Soul winning is a characteristic aftereffect (natural result) of the Christian life. Those who follow Jesus Christ need others to follow Him moreover. Shockingly, many feel deficient in arrangement albeit on edge (anxious) to share their faith. Others feel an absence of certainty, confidence to speak up for Jesus Christ for dread they will neglect to answer the protests or reactions (objections or criticisms).

Also, still others need to express the joy of their abundant life (their Saved Life) in Jesus Christ however would prefer not to lose their companions, friends or shut themselves out from social relationships.

Soul winning and bringing the Good News of salvation through faith and the Lord Jesus Christ is likewise the last prerequisite of the Savior to all of His church. "Go ye into all the world and declare, proclaim, report, preach the Gospel."

1. It is the responsibility of every Christian. He is called to speak to and present Jesus Christ. (II Corinthians 5:19-20 NIV; John 17:18-20 NIV).

2. It is the main answer for the transgression (sin) and despondency (unhappiness) of humanity and the only path for reconciliation with God for eternal life (Romans 6:23 KJV; John 3:36 KJV).

3. It is a gained and learned experience, leading others to salvation (Mark 1:17 NIV; I Peter 3:15 NIV).

4. It is conceivable to win others to Jesus Christ anyplace, anywhere individuals are (John 4:6 NIV; Matthew 28:19 NIV).

5. It is constantly done with the early preparation and full cooperation with God Himself in the Holy Spirit (John 16:7 KJV; I John 2:27 KJV).

6. It is God's will and desire that everyone accept (believe) and not die in everlasting partition from God (II Peter 3:9 KJV; Luke 9:56 KJV).

Methods And Teaching On Soul Winning

No METHOD OR TEACHING on soul winning is perfect for everybody. This applies without clarification. However, an excessive number of Christians are searching for the ideal technique. That method is best when it falls into place without any issues from the longing of any Christian to introduce his faith in Jesus Christ in such a way that others accept and believe likewise in the Savior and follow Him.

Discipleship

DISCIPLESHIP IS NEVER SOLO. Every disciple, with others, pursued Jesus Christ and were His church. Soul winning is in every case progressively powerful if similarly committed people will concur together to start to inform others concerning Jesus Christ.

These recommendations in this manner may give another activity in the "specialty of fishing for people" and make everyone "shine as the stars of the heavens" as well as fulfill the promise of God, "the individual that wins souls will wind up wise" (Proverbs 11:30 KJV).

Steps To Follow

1. Start to pray that you experience recharged, renewed responsibility to your Lord (I Peter 3:15 NIV). Ask God "to bless your heart and make you prepared" to verbalize your faith.

2. Make a list of other people who may start with you this quest for God-like-ness and soul winning despite the fact that now you are not sure with regards to the process or result.

3. Tell your pastor, minister, or spiritual leader of your commitment. Church-focused evangelism is the Biblical method for soul winning. The congregation is designed by God to build up the believers for service and to preserve and mature them in the faith.

4. Study the personal evangelism study course for soul winning. Follow every one of the sacred writings (scriptures) that help the course. Take every passage devoutly requesting that the Lord help you believe and trust it and accomplish it for yourself.

5. Compose a day by day journal or diary of the impressions you get from your study. Ask yourself continually how or what you are accepting can be connected promptly in your endeavors to share your faith.

6. List who you know who you might most want to be saved. These might be seen as more troublesome than others however list those for whom you ought to be prayerfully mindful.

7.   Begin to pray to God for their salvation. Make it your aim that each time you check the time you will make sure to petition God for every one. "Now is the acceptable time, the day of salvation" (I Corinthians 6:2 KJV).

8.   Carry a gospel tract or a little part of sacred text (scripture) with you to be "prepared dependably to give the reason behind the hope" that is yours in Christ. Envision the opening to share what the examination course has prepared you for (I Peter 3:15).

9.   Attempt at every opportunity, as you sense the prompting of God's Holy Spirit, to share your faith and ask that the person receive Jesus Christ as Savior and Lord. Anticipate that God should do great things. You are not the alone in your witness (John 1:12 NIV).

10. Keep in mind that "those that honor God, God will honor," You are doing God's work, with God's Word, in God's way, in God's will.

The first command of the Lord Jesus Christ was "Follow me...I will make you to become fishers of men." His last command was "Go into all the world and preach the Gospel to every creature."

"May the Grace of the Lord Jesus Christ and the love for God and the communion of the Holy Spirit be with you all." Amen.

Reverend Dr. John Thomas Wylie

Study Notes

Study Notes

Chapter
ONE

The Soul Winner's Qualifications

The Purpose

To IDENTIFY AND EXPLAIN the spiritual prerequisites for the effective witness of the Gospel. "He that wins souls is wise" (Proverbs 11:30 KJV). Study to show yourself approved unto God a workman that needeth not to be ashamed, rightly dividing the word of truth" (II Timothy 2:15 KJV).

He should be confident of his own salvation by faith in Jesus Christ. A person in doubt or in uncertainty on any inquiry can't be convincing. There is a fundamental relationship between assurance and witnessing. Because numerous Christians have questions with respect to their salvation, they are hesitant to discuss or speak of it (John 5:24 NIV; I John 5:12 NIV).

Assurance (based on three premises)

a. The Word Of God
    - Faith is essentially "trusting God." (Taking God at His Word).
    - "These things have I written...that ye may "know" that ye have eternal life," (I John 5:13 KJV).
    - "Verily, verily, I say unto you, he that heareth My word and believeth on Him that sent Me "hath everlasting life," (John 5:24 NIV). "Hath equals with "has," which is present tense. Jesus Christ expresses

that upon believing a person is saved "now" and "until the end of time (forever)."
- The Word of God settles doubts.
- Sins are forgiven (Ephesians 1:7 KJV; Acts 26:18 KJV). "And their sins and iniquities will I remember no more," (Hebrews 10:17 KJV).
- Salvation truly secured. (Hebrews 10:12,14 KJV; I John 1:7 KJV; Revelation 1:5 KJV).
- Salvation is eternal.
  "Perfected forever" (Hebrews 10:14 KJV)
  "Shall never perish" (John 10:28 NIV)
  "Sealed unto the day of redemption" (Ephesians 4:30 KJV)
- Fear of failure is a denial of God's promise
  "God is faithful" (I Corinthians 10:13 RSV).
  "Kept by the power of God" (I Peter 1:5 KJV).
  "We have an Advocate when we sin" (I John 2:1 NIV).
  Jesus Christ ever liveth to make intercession for us" (Hebrews 7:25 NIV).

b. The Holy Spirit Assures Of Salvation (Romans 8:16 RSV)
c. God's will, Romans 8:14, is evident by an obedience and a transformed life.

Assurance Results In Witnesses

(NOTE CASES OF ASSURANCE in the Bible and how this assurance resulted in a witness)

a. The strength (boldness) of Peter and John (Acts 4:13 NIV).
- "We can't but speak the things we have "seen" and "heard" (Acts 4:20 KJV).

Dr. John Thomas Wylie

- filled with the Holy Spirit, they spoke the Word of God with boldness (Acts 4:31 KJV).
- "With great power gave the apostles "witness" of the resurrection of the Lord Jesus" (Acts 4:33 NIV).

b. Paul met, heard, and believed on Jesus Christ (Acts 9:1-21 NIV).
    - Filled with the Spirit, he witnessed (Acts 9:17-20 KJV).
    - He stated, "I know whom I have believed" (II Timothy 1:12 KJV).

c. Our gospel came not unto you in word only but also in power and in the Holy Spirit, and in "much assurance" (I Thessalonians 1:5 NIV). This brought about a church that willingly suffered, verse 6, and witnessed, verse 8.

He Must Be Spirit-filled
(Ephesians 5:18 NIV)

THE BODY OF THE believer is the sanctuary (temple) of the Holy Spirit (I Corinthians 6:19 NIV).

1. He should be emptied of every single "unholy" spirit. In the event that a person is to be filled with the Spirit, the seven spirits referenced in Luke 9 must be thrown out (cast out).
    - The careless spirit (verse 33)
    - The prayerless spirit (verse 40)
    - The insensible, ignorant spirit (verse 45)
    - The selfish spirit (verse 46)
    - The sectarian spirit (verse 49)
    - The malevolent, vindictive spirit (verse 54)

- The apathetic, half-hearted spirit (verses 61, 62).

2. The Christian needs the Spirit
   - For power to carry on with the Christian life (Galatians 2:20 NIV)
   - To be kept (I Peter 1:5 KJV, Micah 3:8 KJV)
   - For direction, guidance (Acts 8:29 KJV)
   - For service, especially witness bearing (Acts 1:8; 4:31 KJV; Philippians 2:14-16 KJV; Psalm 51:10-13 KJV. The Holy Spirit gives boldness and power for service and testimony. Compare Acts 2:14-41 KJV; 4:8-12, 29-31 KJV with Matthew 26:58, 69-75 KJV).

The Spirit-filled individual will be yielded to the Spirit's control. The Spirit needs a channel, a voice. The Spirit is the laborer, while the individual is the instrument. Self-will blocks God's work.

He should be a person of persevering prayer. The individual must pray steadily, always. Supplication is the most dismissed benefit of the average believer. There are incalculable impediments that Satan uses to keep us from fellowship with our Lord.

There is a close relationship between prayer and witnessing. Prayer must be as essential as witnessing. Sacred writing (scripture) shows us the relationship of these factors.

1. Subjects For Prayer.
   - Prayer for workers (Matthew 9:37 NIV, 38; John 17:18 NIV).
     God make the inquiry, "Who will go?" (Isaiah 6:8 NIV).
     God is searching for an individual (I Samuel 3:10 NIV; Ezekiel 22:30 NIV).

Dr. John Thomas Wylie

For calling and naming a witness (Acts 1:22-24 NIV; 10:9 NIV; 13:2 NIV; 16:9 NIV; 29:15 NIV).

Viability (effectiveness) of workers in their witness (John 17:33 NIV).

- Prayer for the ministry of ourselves as well as other people.

Such petition is earnestly needed. "Be steadfast" (Acts 6:4 NIV) Prayer aides (helpers) (II Corinthians 1:11 NIV, Ephesians 6:18 NIV,19; Philippians 1:19 NIV).

- Prayer for the unsaved.

For all men, since Jesus Christ gave Himself a ransom for all (I Timothy 2:1-6 NIV).

For the individuals who mistreat, or persecute us (Jeremiah 29:7 NIV; Matthew 5:44 NIV; Acts 7:60 NIV).

For the salvation of the Jews (Romans 10:1 KJV).

2. In witnessing the soul winner must ask God:
   - To lead him to the heart of people to whom He wishes him to talk.
   - To set up the heart of the heathen (sinner) for the message.
   - To guide and bring to remembrance the parts of His Word He wishes to use for each situation. Any accomplished worker will affirm that he has been guided by the Spirit to utilize Scripture that appeared to be most distant from his mind, yet was actually what was required.
   - To offer power to recognize exactly where the trouble, difficulty lies or what the genuine complaints or objections are.

- To give power to what is said. Human reason won't change over the sinner. Simply citing Scripture won't win him. God's power is the main means by which the soul winner can succeed.
- To finish the work and be reliable (consistent) in followup.

3. Prayer prompts total reliance on God.
    For results:
    - "Salvation is of the Lord." The powerful witness will be yielded that the Holy Spirit can guide him to the heart God will open (Acts 16:14 KJV).
    - Pray to God to send the individuals who would benefit from outside intervention and repel the individuals who would not have benefited from outside intervention.
    - While the disciples were praying, the Lord spoke and coordinated (directed) their witness(Acts 10:9; 13:2 KJV).

    For Opportunities To Witness.
    - God prompts people (he leads to individuals) (Acts 2:42 NIV; 3:1 NIV; 16:13 NIV; 16:25 NIV).
    - For boldness to witness (Acts 4:13; 4:29-31 NIV).

4. Examples of Intercessors.
    Abraham, pleading for Sodom (Genesis 18:22,23 NIV).
    Moses, interceding for Israel (Exodus 32:32 NIV)
    Samuel, I Samuel 12:23. Sin stops prayer.
    Daniel, a great intercessor for Israel (Daniel 9:1-23 NIV).

Christ, praying for His Executioners (Luke 23:34 NIV).

Paul (Romans 9:1-3 NIV).

Memory Verses: John 15:7; 20:31; Ephesians 2:8,9; 6:17,19; I John 5:12,13).

Chapter One Questions:

"How Did You Rate?"

1. For what reason is assurance of salvation so vital for powerful witnessing?

2. What is one of the primary reasons why a believer lacks assurance?

3. In what three different ways does God give the believer confirmation (assurance) of salvation?

4. For what reason are sentiments (feelings) a problematic pointer of assurance of salvation?

5. What does it mean to be filled with the Holy Spirit?

6. Name three unholy spirits from which the believer must be purged so as to be filled with the Spirit.

7. What are the three subjects for which the soul winner may pray?

8. Name three Bible characters who were remarkable for their supplication service, particularly intercession.

What do you Think - Yes or No?

_____ An individual who is really saved will know so by the positive sentiment in his heart.

_____It has been stated, "If you can't go, send somebody." Accordingly, conciliatory providing for missions is worthy substitute for individual soul winning.

_____Assurance is the foundation for boldness in witnessing.

_____A sensational or surprising salvation experience is critical if the Christian is to be a successful witness.

_____Moses in begging God for Israel said he thought of it as a sin to stop praying to God for them.

Application

Relate your most recent soul-witnessing knowledge and experience.

What obstructions to witnessing did God enable you to survive?

What verses did you use?

What might you have done any other way?

Study Notes

Study Notes

Chapter
TWO

Jesus Christ's Method
Of Soul Winning

Purpose Of The Lesson

1. To study the method Jesus Christ employed in dealing
    with an individual -
    The Soul Winner himself.
    The Barriers to overcome.
    Jesus Christ's approach and presentation of the gospel.

2. Study Assignment.
    Read John 4 and meditate on it until you are familiar
    with its content.

3. The soul-winner himself.
    1. Three elements of the soul-winner are suggested in
        verse 4: Motivation - - must.
        This motivation compelled Him. Positively this
        was love, for each activity of our Savior from His
        incarnation until his ascension was motivated by
        "Love".
    -   Movement- - "Go."
        He went to the needy soul. Going witnesses prove to
        be fruitful. Hesitant Christians whine that they never
        appear to have openings. Those who look for an open
        entryway find open hearts behind the entryways.
    -   Mission - "Through Samaria."
        He went where others did not go. Paul wanted to
        preach where others had not preached, Virgin soil is a
        good spot to plant seed.

4. Jesus Christ witnessed under adverse conditions.
   - He was physically drained from a long adventure, as well as hungry and thirsty.
   - It was hot and dusty. It was the 6th hour of the day, or high noon.
   - He stood up to the social and cultural differences.

5. Jesus ministered in view of need in mind.
   - Other ladies came early or late in the day.
   - This woman's social dismissal is proposed by her coming around noon and alone.
   - Jesus Christ knew this and met her alone when it would least humiliate her.

6. Barriers To Overcome.
   A. Barrier of prejudice. There was an extreme scorn among Jews and Samaritans, verse 9. The ruler set her in a predominant position by influencing Himself to rely on her. He asked her assistance. She reacted. he illustrated (a) humility; (b) concern; (c) dependence; (d) tact. This totally incapacitated her. never go to the unbeliever in pride.
   B. Barrier of sex. "How is it...a "woman of Samaria" verse 9. Custom would manage this contact to not be right. It is best for men to work with men; ladies with ladies. The Holy Spirit must be perceived as sovereign. "Man's ways are not God's ways."
   C. Barrier of ignorance. "If thou knewest, verse 10. The woman was oblivious of the blessing (gift) and the Giver. Her advantage was excited at the possibility of a blessing (gift). Jesus Christ was not ransacking her but rather offering her what she hungered for and truly needed"living water."

Dr. John Thomas Wylie

D. Barrier of sin. "Go, call thy husband," verses 16-18. The issue of how to enable the individual face to sin is constantly troublesome. Judge not. The Holy Spirit will uncover the condition, John 16:7-9. People in sin fear the light. They should be pulled in to Christ first. In His essence sin winds up show. The woman is on edge and inquisitive however not yet prepared for the endowment of eternal life and forgiveness until she faces her sin.

E. Barrier of religion. "Our fathers worshiped in this mountain..." verses 19-24. She needed to make a contention over the place of worship. He rapidly put this aside and went to the heart. Try not to win individuals to a religion, however to a person, the Lord Jesus. God isn't worried about structure or function, form or ceremony, but with heart faith.

7. The Approach-- from the known to the unknown, a law of learning.
   1. He began with water and continued to living water.

   2. He requested that her exhibit what she could do- - draw water, and told her what He could do- - produce a well of water.

   3. Her water would result in thirst. His brought about thirst satisfied.

   4. Her water would continue real life. His delivered eternal life.

8. The Procedure
   1. The perspective on the average individual is:

- Proud, verse 9.
- Ignorant, verse 10.
- Unsatisfied, verse 15
- Sinful, verse 18.
- Deceived, verse 22.

2. Note the four stages by which Jesus Christ was perceived by the woman.
   - A Jew, verse 9. Back of this is a lifetime of dealings which have heightened her disdain. A Jew viewed himself as unclean if the shadow of a Samaritan fell on him. Today most of humanity sees no more in Christ than that He is a noteworthy figure.
   - Sir, verse 11. His thoughtfulness and refusal to react in kind to her frame of mind marks Him as an honorable man. She currently has picked up respect. Her consideration is moved from the complaints to her experience.
   - Prophet, verse 19. She is faced with omniscience, the attribute of God. The Word of God does this to each sinner.
   - The Messiah, verses 25-29. Her depiction of the Messiah turns into the methods for ID. He had "revealed to her all things." She comes back to her people in the town to tell everybody.
   Memory Verses: Jeremiah 17:9; Luke 19:10; John 5:24; I Corinthians 3:11; Galatian 3:13 KJV.

Chapter Two Study Questions

How Did You Rate?

1. How do the words "motivation," "movement," and "mission" depict Jesus Christ in John 4, in managing the woman at the well?

2. Under what adverse conditions did Jesus Christ witness to this woman?

3. With what barrier of sin did Jesus Christ deal?

4. What was the barrier of prejudice which Jesus Christ overcame?

5. What was the barrier of religion? What lesson do we gain from themanner in which Jesus Christ managed it?

6. What law of learning did Jesus see in managing the woman?

7. Jesus Christ was uncovered to the woman by what four stages?

What Do You Think - Yes Or No?

_____ The barrier of religion is often experienced by the witness since numerous individuals in this nation are very religious, however unsaved.

_____ In perspective on the instructive accomplishments in this land, a great many people are very proficient with respect to the Bible. Accordingly, ignorance is one boundary that will more often than not be experienced.

_____ Jesus Christ speedily identified Himself to the woman at the well as the Messiah so she would know about to whom she was talking.

_____ A sinner isn't prepared to get the endowment of eternal life until he has been made to confront his sin.

_____ Jesus Christ managed the woman with the most extreme cordiality and graciousness until her sin of having had five spouses became known.

Study Notes

Study Notes

Chapter

THREE

Opportunities For Witness: How To Begin

1. Expectancy

    The way (key) to circumstances in witnessing is "expectancy." Be constantly alert. This "expectancy" will be communicated in two different ways:

    1. A concern for individuals. We see it in Jesus Christ, Luke 19:10, "to seek and to save, "For necessity is laid upon me; yea, woe is me if I preach not the Gospel" (I Corinthians 9:16.

    2. A concern for the purpose of the Holy Spirit. "Ye shall be witnesses" (Acts 1:8. Ephesians 5:16, "Redeeming the time because the days are evil." Take preferred standpoint of each opportunity. They might be gone rapidly. Catch them when they occur. This requires consistent expectancy.

2. Guidelines For Opportunities.
    1. Try not to constrain opportunities. Some ask, "To whom am I to speak?" To everybody whom God sends you. Why not address each one? Do as such if God prompts you to do as such. Keep in mind God makes our chances (opportunities). This should cause everyone to be set up by the Holy Spirit with the goal that when openings (opportunities) come you will be yielded to the control of the Spirit, and prepared for God's opportunities.
        -   Much prayer concerning openings (opportunities) (Acts 10:9,34).

- Meditation on God's Word. "Live in the Word." (Psalm 119:105).
- Readiness by permitting no deterrents in our lives (I Peter 3:15).
- Yielding to the Holy Spirit's totality (Holy Spirit's fullness) (Mark 1:17).
- Cultivating a frame of mind of attentive hope (watchful expectation) (I Peter 3:15; Acts 16:31; Romans 1:15; I Corinthians 16:9).

2. Try not to pass up on chances (Do not miss opportunities).
   We should remember that open doors may come (Opportunity):
   - Any place. Openings (opportunities) can be found anyplace individuals are available.

     Jesus Christ addressed the hoodlum (thief) while they were both on the cross.
   - Any time. Openings (again opportunities) may come at any hour of the day or night. We ought to be on the alert for somebody who has heard the Word and whose heart is set up by the Spirit for a choice.
   - Any individual. Personal evangelism offers the chance to meet individuals in different social statuses. Jesus witnessed to fishermen, publicans, outcasts, lepers, scribes, Pharisees, Saduccees, soldiers, rulers, adulterers, and so forth.

3. We Are God's Ambassadors.
   "ambassadors for Jesus Christ" (II Corinthians 5:20). We are "designated" (delegated) by God to do personal work. The Spirit is making openings and indicting

(convicting) the world. He is driving us to somebody who will respond. We should meet the arrangements the Lord has set up for us.

4. Tact Is Essential

    Tact is fundamental in opening a discussion. Contact is tact incorporated. Tact is important for the methodology (approach). It ought to be developed. The Holy Spirit will control us as we make our methodology (approach). Numerous Christians are excluded due to lack of tact.

5. Too Aspects of Contact.
    1. With God. The supplication life of the soul winner can't be over-emphasized. Keep in mind that there can be no work achieved apart from fellowship with God. James 1:5 is the wellspring of wisdom.

        With man. This is personal work. The Holy Spirit must have unlimited authority, complete control. "We have this treasure in earthen vessels that the excellency of the power may be of God and not of us." (II Corinthians 4:7).

6. Three Hindrances In Contacts With Sinners
    1. Abruptness. It will frequently close the open door as opposed to opening it more extensively. Be an audience (a listener).

    2. Argument. This is removing the work from God's hands and endeavoring to get a choice by human astuteness. Nobody was ever saved by contention (Argument). Argument will regularly prompt

individual comments which lead to hostility. We are witnesses, not debaters.

3.   Antagonism. This will close the way to future chances (opportunities). Antagonism frequently becomes out of analysis of denominations, houses of worship, ministers, pastors, people, and social relations. The soul winner ought to maintain a strategic distance from any analysis in managing the unsaved. Witness boldly concerning Jesus Christ. People may abandon Him (John 1:11) but we ought to never neglect to keep our discussion on Jesus Christ and the issues of salvation.

7.   Two Helps In Making Contacts
1.   Be Open. At Ease. Make individuals feel calm (at ease). Contact is dependent upon methodology (approach). Make the inquiries: When you address others about their soul, do they hesitate to address you? Do you appear to hurl boundaries or barriers that disallow them from addressing you? Is it true that you are acting and talking normally?

2.   Be Persistent. A few people are dependably on edge. We ought not be excessively on edge and not easily discouraged. Go the extent that you can without inconvenience (annoyance).

8.   Suggested Steps To Be Used In The Approach
1.   Put The Inquirer At Ease With A Personal Question. Use class in making an inquiry. "What church do you visit?" not "Do you go to church?" The soul winner's inquiry should draw out the seeker instead of

causing withdrawal. An inquiry which has a suggested allegation or judgment in it is the wrong approach.

2. Begin on a shared opinion of conversation (or discussion). Get the inquirer to talk. Be a decent audience (a good listener) and stay away from the "bad habit of chattiness." The conversation can regularly be begun by making an inquiry about what is of highest enthusiasm (what interests the inquirer most).

3. Use an expression of personal testimony to present the subject of salvation.

4. Find where the individual is. Find his inconvenience and felt need. See Acts 13:9-10 KJV.

5. Rephrase the Word of God. Instances of tact are found in Acts 6 and I Corinthians 9:19.

9. Be Ready - take advantage of openings. Romans 1:15 KJV).
   1. Some will inquire. (I Peter 3:15 KJV).

   2. Others will be readied (prepared). (Acts 8:30; 10:33 KJV).

   3. Afflictions (Pains) will open the entryway. (Mark 5:28 KJV).

   4. Circumstances will set up the way (Mark 5:33 KJV).

   5. The nearness or presence of death stirs or awakes people (John 11:45 KJV).

6. A Casual remark (easygoing comment) by a person will give a contact and opening.
    Memory Verses: Psalm 66:18, Proverbs 27:1; John 10:9, Romans 10:9-10; II Corinthians 6:2; Hebrews 11:6 KJV.

Chapter Three Study Questions

How Did You Rate?

1. What are two vital parts of contact?

2. What are some common grounds on which a discussion with an unsaved individual may start.

3. Three hindrances to displaying the gospel must be maintained a strategic distance from (be avoided). What are they?

4. For what reason should our talk dependably be focused on Jesus Christ and the Word of God?

5. Name three circumstances which can offer open doors for exhibiting the gospel.

6. What is the key to open doors (opportunities) for witnessing?

7. What two frames of mind in a Christian will create readiness (alertness) to open doors for witnessing?

8. How might prepare himself for circumstances (opportunities) which God makes for witnessing? It would be ideal if you recommend three different ways.

9. What is the most worthwhile occasions (advantages times) for doing personal work?

10. Give two scriptural examples of believers who were explicitly sent to witness to someone.

What Do You Think - Yes or No?

- Salvation is an actual life and death issue. A grave, calm face is, hence, critical to pass on the seriousness of our witness.
- Persistence in witnessing ought to be avoided as a great many people would be aggravated.
- A good procedure for introducing salvation is to give your personal testimony.
- Unless a Christian has undergrided his existence with supplication, his witness will achieve close to little or nothing.
- Since we are to be occupied "in season and out of season," it is incumbent on the soul winner to make every contact with someone else an open door for witnessing.
- "Redeeming the time" signifies to take advantage all open doors for witnessing.
- The conditions of Paul meeting with the Ethiopian Eunuch is a good example of how one can be sent of God to an unsaved person.
- Some Christians have little open door (opportunity) for witnessing, when they are wiped out in a medical clinic, or bound.
- The last recorded witness of Jesus Christ brought about the change of the centurion who stood underneath the cross.

Application

Appeal to God for wisdom to perceive open doors (opportunities) for witnessing, and boldness to take advantage of them.

Dr. John Thomas Wylie

Chapter

FOUR

How To Present The Gospel

Man Is A Sinner, And Therefore Guilty.

1. Purpose Of The Lesson
    - To bring people to faith in Jesus Christ, an individual should obviously and consistently present the need for Christ, and the arrangement (provision) God has made to address that need. While there are numerous methodologies, this exercise puts forward the plain certainties, and the straightforwardness of the effortlessness or simplicity of the gospel.

2. The Gospel Is Reasonable And logical
    - God's welcome or invitation to the sinner is to "Come and reason," Isaiah 1:18. God utilizes sound (reasonable) and legitimate (logical) thinking to persuade men regarding their sin and demonstrate to them the truth of their reality. It ought to be our purposes to so comprehend God's Word that we will most likely present it in the equivalent coherent, straightforward and engaging way. There is an unmistakable plan for presenting the Gospel.

3. Four Steps In Presenting The Gospel
    Scripture verses on salvation can be orchestrated into four gatherings which give an example empowering the individual (soul winner) to continue logically.
    - All are sinners and therefore in need a Savior.
    - Without Jesus Christ they are blameworthy, guilty, condemned, and without hope.

- Jesus Christ died, was buried, and rose again that all might be saved.
- God's salvation can be received just only as a gift, by accepting, without credit or human exertion.

4. The Importance Of Orderly Presentation
    In the event that three and four are introduced before one and two, the Holy Spirit can't bring the conviction that is fundamental before an individual will want to receive Jesus Christ. Many will promptly admit they are sinners with little concept of the penalty of sin.

5. All Are Sinners In Need Of A Saviour
    1. Confront The Sinner With This Fact. This is comprehensive, faced by each person. "All," "none," and "not one," in Romans 3:9-12. Romans 3:23, "For all": in Isaiah 53:6, "All we like sheep have gone astray"; in Galatians 3:22, "All under sin." Salvation is a personal issue since sin is a personal issue.

    2. Seek To Show The Sinful Their lost Condition
        Seek to show the sinful their lost condition of the person as soon as possible. This is outlined in Nathan's discussion with David in II Samuel 12:7; additionally, Jesus with the Scribes and Pharisees in John 8:7; Jesus with Nicodemus in John 3:7; and with the woman at the well in John 4:18.

    3. Seven Scriptural Definitions Of Sin.
        -   Coming short (falling short, coming up short, missing the mark) of the glory of God (Romans 3:23).

Dr. John Thomas Wylie

- Going astray, turning to our own way (Isaiah 53:6).
- Transgression of the law, I John 3:4. The breaking of God's commandments. Note Matthew 22:37-39 as a synopsis of the Ten Commandments. Demonstrate that the reason for the law in Romans 3:20 was to give knowledge of sin. The law was not given to save. Use Romans 1:29-32 to demonstrate God's attitude toward the wicked, sinful acts of men.
- All unrighteousness is sin, (I John 5:17).
- Sin is neglect, inability to make the right decision (to do what is right) (James 4:17).
- Sin is doing doubtful things (Romans 14:23). Leaves a feeling of remorse, a guilty conscience.
- Sin is unbelief in Jesus Christ (John 16:8-9).

4. All Men Are Sinners Separated From God:
   Since all men are sinners, humankind is isolated from God (Isaiah 59:2). The principal demonstration of sin was to look to maintain a strategic distance from the presence of God (Genesis 3:8). Jesus Christ clarifies this in John 3:19-21. The gospel is a good news of reconciliation (II Corinthians 5:18-20).

5. Emphasis Placed On The Holy Spirit's Convicting Of Sin.
   Emphasis should be placed upon the Holy Spirit's convicting men for sin, the transgression (sin) of unbelief. Jesus Christ came to save sinners. Each sinner needs the Savior (John 16:8-9).

6. Mankind must recognize he is a powerless, helpless sinner.
   - Man is dead in trespasses and sins (Ephesians 2:2).
   - Man can't change (Jeremiah 13:23; John 8:31-36; Ephesians 2:3).
   - God requires perfection in law keeping (James 2:10).
   - Man can't work his way out (Romans 4:4-5; Ephesians 2:8-10).
   - Man has no righteousness (Isaiah 64:6; Romans 10:3).
   - No earthly cleaner will reach man's heart (Jeremiah 10:23, Romans 8:7-8; Galatians 2:16, 20; Titus 3:5).

7. All Without Christ Are Children Of The Devil.
   A very common assumption is the universal fatherhood of God. (Romans 8:9; 9:8. Cautiously examine the Scriptures:
   - Children of the Devil (John 8:44; Acts 13:10; I John 3:8-10).
   - Children of the Wicked one (II Samuel 7:10; Job 41:34; Isaiah 1:4; 30:9; 57:4; Ephesians 2:2-3; t:6; Luke 16:8; Matthew 13:38; 23:15; II Peter 2:14).

8. In God's Eyes Mankind Is Depraved And Polluted
   Man is completely depraved and polluted as seen by God:
   Read what God says in the Scripture about each part of man's inner and outer body parts:
   - Head (Isaiah 1:15).
   - Eyes (II Peter 2:14).
   - Mouth (Romans 3:14).

Dr. John Thomas Wylie

- Lips (Romans 3:13).
- Tongue (Romans 3:13).
- Throat (Romans 3:13).
- Neck (Deuteronomy 31:27).
- Ears (Matthew 13:15).
- Hands (Psalm 26:10).
- Feet (Romans 3:15).
- Head to Foot (Isaiah 1:6).
- Bones (Job 20:11).
- Inward Parts (Psalm 5:9).
- Mind (Romans 1:28).
- Thoughts (Genesis 6:5).
- Understanding (Ephesians 4:18).
- Heart (Jeremiah 17:9).
- Conscience (I Timothy 4:2).
- Feeling (Ephesians 4:19).
- Way (Romans 3:16,17).
- Nature (Ephesians 4:22).

9. A Word Of Compassion.

   John 3:17 demonstrates that Jesus Christ did not come to condemn but rather to save. Give us a chance to take care not to take every necessary step of the Holy Spirit. Give the person a chance to read the Scriptures. The Scriptures are the Sword of the Spirit. Similarly as an individual ends up mindful of a feared physical sickness and after that looks for a medical specialist, so a person who ends up mindful of sin will perceive a need of Christ.

   Try not to preach to the sinner. Join yourself to him. Try not to say, "You are a sinner." Rather, "God plainly reveals that we as a whole are sinners and, in this way, need a Savior.

1. Without Jesus Christ "ALL" Are Guilty, Condemned, And Sentenced.
    1. The Four Results Of Sin:
        - All sinners are abominable to God (Deuteronomy 25:16; Proverbs 8:7; 15:9,26; 16:5 NIV.
        - Separates from God here and hereafter. (Genesis 3:3; 4:16; Isaiah 59:2; Hebrews 1:13 NIV.
        - Brings death. (Ezekiel 18:4; Romans 5:12; 6:23; James 1:15) NIV.
        - God punishes sin. (Isaiah 13:11; Amos 3:2 NIV).

    2. The Penalty Of Sin Is Punishment
        - Death (Physical And Spiritual)
            a. Death is the detachment of an individual from the purpose or use for which he was made.
            b. As utilized in Romans 6:23, death incorporates:
        - Physical Death (Romans 5:12; I Corinthians 15:21,22; Hebrews 9:27 NIV).
        - Spiritual Death or Separation of the spirit (soul) from God.
            The spiritual existence of the unsaved is secured by "trespasses and sins" and is along these lines rendered inadequate or incapable of knowing and enjoying God. (Ephesians 2:1; 4:18; I Timothy 5:6; I John 3:14; 5:12; Revelation 3:1 NIV).

        - Eternal Death or Eternal Separation from God. (II Thessalonians 1:19; I Corinthians 5:9,10; Matthew 25:30,41,46 NIV).

Dr. John Thomas Wylie

c. Death Is Never Annihilation, or Destruction in the feeling of annihilation. Have a go at substituting annihilation and see the inconceivability in such verses as Mark 14:1,34; Romans 5:10; Luke 8:52,53 NIV; Romans 6:2,8; I John 3:14. The sinner is said to be dead while living (Ephesians 2:1; I Timothy 5:6 NIV). Death is the nonappearance (absence) of life and spiritual death is the nonattendance (absence) of Jesus Christ, Who is the life. Death is, along these lines expulsion (banishment) from God. (I John 5:12; John 17:3; Colossians 3:14; I Corinthians 6:9,10; II Thessalonians 1:8,9. The Second Death, the penalty for sin, is in Revelation 21:8, and is eternal. (Revelation 20:10 NIV).

- Hell (Psalm 9:17; Luke 16:23-25,28; Matthew 11:20-24; Luke 10:15; Matthew 5:22;18:8,9; 23:15,22; Mark 9:43-48. See likewise John 3:36; Galatians 6:7,8; Matthew 8:12; II Peter 2:17 NIV.

- Everlasting Punishment. (Jews 6:2; II Thessalonians 1:9; Mark 3:29; Matthew 25:46; Jude 7 KJV).

- The Wrath Of God. (Romans 2:5; John 3:36 KJV).
  Make a rundown (list) of events in the Bible where the wrath of God against sin and the sinner is plainly and clearly defined.

3. The Danger Of The Sinner's Destiny (John 3:18). John clarifies that the getaway from Judgment is

conceivable just for the individuals who have faith in Jesus Christ. People go to Judgment because they reject the Savior. Humankind does not have to effectively be lost. He is lost as of now. Jesus Christ came not to condemn (judge) the world, however that the world through Him may be saved... (John 3:17 KJV).

4. Judgment Is Future. Sacred texts (scriptures) as Romans 5:12; 6:23; and Revelation 21:8 make this unmistakable. In John 8:21-24, Jesus said you will "die in your transgressions." In John 3:36 the individuals who reject Christ are withstanding under the fury (wrath) of God as of now. Accepting and believing in Jesus Christ delivers from (judgment) which is eternal separation from God (John 5:24 KJV).

5. The reality of eternal judgment brings men under spiritual conviction of transgression (sin). Note Acts 24:25; 2:37; and 7:54 KJV. It was Jonathan Edward's renowned message "Sinners in the Hands of an Angry God (Hebrews 10:31)" that moved the huge number to conviction and repentance. John the Baptist was an evangelist of looming judgment (Luke 3:7 KJV).

    The Old Testament prophets nearly no matter what ceaselessly cautioned Israel about the anger of God and the coming Judgment. Note that the service of the Holy Spirit in John 16:8,9 is to convict of sin, righteousness, and judgment. Once more, it is the rejection of Jesus Christ that is principaly in view.

    Memory Verses: John 3:18; Romans 3:9-12; Romans 5:12.

Dr. John Thomas Wylie

Chapter Four Study Questions

How Did You Rate?

1. Give a reference which proposes that God is a sensible God, and needs the sinner to prevail upon Him.

2. With the utilization of your Bible, state what I Peter 3:15 proposes concerning the sensibility of our salvation.

3. What are four intelligent strides in showing the gospel?

4. For what reason is an efficient introduction of the gospel basic?

5. What two references might you be able to propose which express that all have trespassed (sinned)?

6. In managing an inquirer, what should the observer try to do when conceivable?

7. Seven Scriptural definitions are given to sin. If you don't mind give three.

8. In view of Romans 5:12, what is the basic confirmation that all men are sinners?

9. What are two present after-effects of sin? What are two after-death results.

10. What is implied by "death" as it applies to the unsaved people?

What do you Think - Yes or No?

_____ The righteous man is powerless to achieve anything in seeing separated from the service of the Word and the Holy Spirit.

_____ Missing the desire for God's flawlessness could be said to be one meaning of transgression.

_____ An unsaved individual who does not remember he is a sinner won't perceive the need for a Savior.

_____ The main demonstration of Adam subsequent to erring (sinning) was to search out God with an end goal to be accommodated.

_____The just two special cases to the announcement in the Bible, "All have trespassed" were Enoch and Elijah, since they went to paradise without first dying.

_____ The subject of eternal judgment ought to be abstained from amid individual witnessing as it will cause disdain in the unbeliever.

_____ Man turns into a sinner the minute he submits his first sin subsequent to coming to the period of accountability.

_____ Everlasting discipline for the delinquent is a continuation of the wrath of God which presently tolerates on him.

_____ Since Jesus Christ appeared on the scene "not to condemn the world but rather to save it," He painstakingly maintained a strategic distance from the subject of the fury and judgment of God.

Application

Relate an involvement in witnessing. Tell the accompanying:

-   The response of the individual to your observer
-   Objections raised, assuming any
-   What verses you utilized
-   Outcome of your witness
-   Any other interesting details

Study Notes

Study Notes

Chapter
FIVE

How To Share The Gospel

JESUS CHRIST DIED, WAS buried, and rose again that we might be saved.

1. The Substitutionary Work Of Jesus Christ.

     This work is that the foundation upon that the arrange of salvation is constructed. It answers the question, "How will God be simply and therefore the proponent of him United Nations agency believes United Nations agency believes in Jesus?" (Romans 3:6).

-    Savior died as a substitute for the offender. He paid God's judgment for sin. (Isaiah 63:5; First Epistle to the Corinthians 15:3; Hebrews 9:28; 10:12; book 3:18. He bore our sins in His own body. (Isaiah 53:5,6; book 2:24 KJV. He might be our substitute as a result of He was innocent. (II Corinthians 5:21; book 2:22; First Epistle of John 3:5 KJV. He was innocent as a result of he's God's Son - immortal, virgin born. He failed to inherit a sinful attribute (Luke 1:31-36 KJV).

-    He understand that God accepted His finished work as a result of He raised Him from the dead. (Romans 4:24,25; First Epistle to the Corinthians 15:4; Acts 1:3 KJV; the best proof of Christianity (Romans 1:4 KJV); the best exhibition of God's power (Ephesians 1:20 KJV); the best truth of the Gospel (I Corinthians 15:3,4 KJV); the best reality of religion (I Thessalonians 4:14 KJV); the best assurance of returning glory (I Corinthians 15:20 KJV); the best incentive to quality (Romans 6:9-12 KJV)."

2. The death of Savior because the sinner's substitute was the fulfillment of prophecy each in sort and direct revelation.

    -   In forecast. Paul declared in First Epistle to the Corinthians 5:7 KJV, "For even Christ our Passover is sacrificed for US." In Exodus twelve, we've the main points of the substitute. A lamb was to be taken and slain, and therefore the blood wet on the door posts. By religion the individuals took their position within the house. "The blood shall be to you for a token upon the homes wherever ye are; and once I see the blood i will be able to leave out you, and therefore the plague shall not be upon you to destroy you, once I smite the land of Egypt" (Exodus 12:13 KJV). In Hebrews 8-10, we tend to see Savior because the nice anti-type of all the Levitical sacrifices..

    -   In Revelation. (In Isaiah fifty three we tend to scan such statements as "He was wounded for our transgressions." Note Acts 8:28-35 KJV wherever Prince Philip taken this passage to the Ethiopian man.

3. Jesus Christ referred His substitutionary add Mark 10:45. He took His disciples aside on varied occasions to inform them concerning His returning death. He firmly set His face to travel to Jerusalem. On the cross He ended His substitutionary work by oral communication, "It is finished." Notice the mockery in Matthew 27:41-42 KJV, "He saved others' Himself He cannot save." scan Psalm twenty two and sixty nine to review the main points of the crucifixion written by the prophet David a thousand years before the event happened.

4. God's Salvation Received As A Gift Apart From Works. This is the step that brings God's saving. Here the

excellence is created between what man will do and what God has done. The principle is "believing is seeing," not "seeing is believing."

1. God's offer of a free gift is AN obstacle to man. the greatest objection to God's salvation to the human mind is that the sinner is needed to try to to nothing and, indeed, will do nothing to receive it, but believe. The flesh feels it must do one thing. The natural mind doesn't need to believe what God says regarding the flesh, that it's corrupt, sinful, and condemned.

2. Four Facts regarding Salvation.
    -   it's a gift. (John 3:16; 4:10; Romans 3:24 KJV; Second Epistle of Paul the Apostle to the Corinthians 9:15; Ephesians 2:8,9; Revelation 21:6; 22:17 KJV).
    -   it's apart from works or law (anything man will do). (Romans 3:19,20, 28; 4:1-5 KJV; Galatians 2:16 KJV; Ephesians 2:3-10 KJV).
    -   it's on the premise of believing or religion. (Hebrews 11:6. Note additionally John 1:12 KJV; 3:16, 18,36; 5:24).
    -   it's ours just by receiving the person of jesus christ. (John 1:12 KJV; First Epistle of John 5:12 KJV; Revelation 3:20 KJV).

3. Salvation is a matter of regeneration, not reformation.
    -   Man is seen as dead in trespasses and sins. (Ephesians 2:1,2). this implies he doesn't have life or any relationship to God. He wants resurrection from the dead. the same power is needed to avoid wasting him as was needed to lift Redeemer from the dead. (Ephesians 1:20).

- Salvation is that the imparting of life. this is often called:
- a new creation (II Corinthians 5:17 NIV).
- The New Birth (John 1:12,13; 3:1-7 NIV).
- From Death to Life (John 5:2 NIV 4).
- saving from Satans' domain into a new kingdom (Colossians 1:13 NIV).
- A partaker of divine nature (II Peter 1:4 NIV).
- we become the sons of God when we believe. (John 1:12; First Epistle of John 2:29 -3:2 NIV).

4. Elements Of Faith:
   - Facts. man needs the facts and information presented above - that he is a sinner and therefore guilty and condemned; that Jesus Christ died and rose again as a full satisfaction for his sin. He cannot believe without first knowing these facts. How then shall they call on Him in Whom they have not believed? And how shall they believe in Him of Whom they have not heard? (Romans 10:1 NIV 4).
   - Agreement. It is essential that the person seeking to know Christ agrees with these facts. The Spirit of God will use a Scriptural and logical presentation of these truths, and the probability is therefore great that he will believe and be saved.
   - Commitment. The most important aspect in faith is to trust Jesus Christ as the only and perfect Saviour from sin, believing in. His finished work on Calvary as the complete satisfaction for sin. Many will agree with the facts of salvation, but stop short of taking the step of personal commitment to Jesus Christ.

Dr. John Thomas Wylie

They are similar to the person who says, "I Believe that a jet plane is the fastest and even the safest way of traveling, but you'll never catch me in one." Such a person does not, in truth, "believe" in a plane until he steps aboard, and commits himself as a passenger.

Provisionally, the gospel of Jesus Christ which is the power of God unto salvation is for "whosoever will," irrespective of what he or she may be or what he or she may have done. Potentially, it is only to "everyone that believeth.' The sinner takes the position saying, "I believe the promises of God enough to venture an eternity on them."

5. Saving Faith. Ponder the following.
    You may offer like Cain (Genesis 4:3 NIV)

    Weep like Esau (Genesis 27:38 NIV)

    Serve like Gehazi (II Kings 5:20 NIV)

    Leave Sodom like Lot's wife (Genesis 19:26 NIV)

    Tremble like Felix (Acts 24:25 NIV)

    Take part in worship like Korah (Numbers 16:19 NIV)

    Desire to die he death of the righteous like Balaam (Numbers 23:10 NIV)

    Make long prayers like the Pharisees (Matthew 23:14 NIV)

Prophesy like Saul (I Samuel 10:10 NIV)

Have lamps like the foolish virgins (Matthew 25:1-13 NIV)

Be a seeking soul like the rich young ruler (Matthew 19:16 NIV)

Be almost a Christian like Agrippa (Acts 26:28 NIV)

And YET BE LOST.

Memory Verses. John 1:12,29; 10:27-29; I Corinthians 15:3,4.

Study Questions

How Did You Rate?

1. What is the foundation whereupon the plan of salvation is built?

2. How could Christ (one individual) die as a substitute for the numerous transgressions (sins) of the entire world?

3. In what manner would God be able to legitimize (or declare righteous) the believer, and still be just?

4. What is the best reality ever?

5. How was the Passover, celebrated by Israel, an image of Christ's death for the sinner?

6. How does the Bible put forward or portray the all out evil (depravity of) of man?

7. What is the human personality's greatest protest or objection to God's salvation?

8. For what reason can't man add to God's salvation by acts of kindness? (or good works)?

9. What is the teaching of Scripture concerning the universal fatherhood of God regarding as salvation?

10. Name three Scriptural terms which depict salvation as the impartation of life.

What Do You Think - Yes or No?

- The resurrection of Christ from the dead is proof of the acknowledgment by God of the completed work of Christ on Calvary.
- Christ's capture in the Garden of Gethsemane and His consequent torturous killing overwhelmed Him totally and by surprise.
- Scripture pictures man as totally polluted.
- God's guideline is "believing is seeing."
- Salvation is by grace through faith in addition to nothing.
- While it is feasible for the sinner to reform, he won't generally change himself as a sinner.
- An unsaved individual who has attempted to improve himself ethically, stands a superior shot of being saved than a "the dumps push bum."
- a similar power is required to save a sinner as was required to raise Christ from the dead.

Application

Pray, that we may see the surpassing wickedness of transgression (sin), from god's perspective, even in purported "good" individuals. It was this sinfulness that required nothing less than the extreme cure of Christ dying on the cross, and being resurrected.

Study Notes

Study Notes

Chapter
SIX

Many Kinds Of Objectors

1. The Self-Righteous.

   The Self-righteous man believes in God, however He isn't the God of the Bible, but instead a divine being (god) he has produced. Such a divine being (god) is happy with a man who does the best he supposedly can, satisfies the light of his conscience, and by and large is "good." This objector has built up his own standard of righteous nature.

   He is the cutting edge Pharisee (modern day Pharisee) who expresses gratitude toward God that he isn't like other men are. He realizes he isn't impeccable, yet defends that "good" individuals will naturally go to heaven, and he is very happy with his record of being a good "model," a decent individual, "a good role model by earthly guidelines. He has no specific sense of "sin."

   1. A Paramount Question: Can benevolent acts and praiseworthy deeds of man give an adequate premise to acquiring eternal life? Or on the other hand do men need a Savior whose blood rinses from transgression (sin)? Upon what does man's promise for paradise depend? Upon himself or upon Jesus Christ?

   2. Usual answers of self-righteous. Upon request with respect to their salvation, the self-righteous will answer to some degree as pursues:
      - "I am good enough."
      - "I attempt to do right by everyone."
      - "I don't drink."
      - "I keep the law."
      - "I am naturally good."

-    "I am no more worse than others."

3.   God's picture of the self-righteous (Romans 2:1-16 KJV).
-    He is unpardonable, inexcusable (Verse 2,3 KJV).
-    Condemned (Verse 4 KJV).
-    Self-righteous and despised God's goodness, forbearance, and longsuffering (Verse 5).
-    Doomed (Verses 6-11 KJV).
-    Helpless. The conditions whereupon he can be saved without Christ are appeared in this chapter, yet not finding himself perfect in God's sight, he should look to Jesus Christ to save him.

4.   "Do" or "Done"? An expression of two letters depicts the religion of the self-righteous - "do." The gospel message is in a four-letter word - "undone." Jesus stated, It is finished" (John 19:30 KJV. The self-righteous gets rid of the expression of Jesus Christ. If a man can save himself, Christ died in vain (Galatians 2:21 KJV).

5.   Perfect righteousness is absolutely essential. To be saved, to show up within the presence of a heavenly God, man must have a perfect righteousness. In what manner can man procure it since he doesn't have it? Read what God declares about our righteousness in the accompanying Scriptures: Isaiah 64:6; Romans 3:9-20 KJV.

6.   Righteousness isn't by the law or keeping it. (Romans 3:20.21,28; 4:13-15; Galatians 3:11 KJV).

7. Righteousness isn't by works (Romans 4:5; 3:27; Titus 3:5 KJV).

- If one could earn salvation by works, God would owe it to him as an obligation (Romans 4:4,5 KJV).

- Salvation isn't "BY" works, "for' works. (Romans 10:3 explains why men endeavor to contend and reason, and reason themselves.

- God demonstrates His objection to fills in as a means of approval in His sight. Note Cain (Genesis 4:5; Saul (I Samuel 15:23 KJV).

- God views the heart, not upon acts (I Samuel 16:7; Proverbs 16:2; 30:12; Isaiah 64:6; Jeremiah 17:9,10; Luke 16:15; Philippians 3:9 KJV. Cautiously audit Luke 18:10-14 as for the self-righteous.

- Scripture indicates instances of good men needing salvation.
  Nicodemus (John 3:3 KJV)
  Cornelius (Acts 10:1-6; 11:1'1-14 KJV)
  Paul (Philippians 3:4-8 KJV).

8. Righteousness is by Faith. (Galatians 3:20; 2:16; Romans 1:16,17 3:22; Hebrews 11:6 KJV. We can satisfy God by "faith as it were." (John 6:28,29; Hebrews 11:6).

2. The Indifferent And The Unconcerned.

About the hardest individual to manage is the unconcerned one. Typically this kind of individual trusts in personal morality. He may have all the material needs of life. "Healthy, well off, and wise," is the thing that he may state. Or on the other hand "Everything is lovely and for what reason would it be advisable for me to be concerned?"

1. Try to identify the conviction of sin and need of forgiveness. (Isaiah 53:6; Romans 3:23). Show all persons a sinner is helpless, condemned and unacceptable to God's expectation.

2. Guilt before God is obvious.
-   breaking the first commandment (Matthew 22:37,38 KJV).
-   Rejecting Jesus Christ (John 16:7-9; 3:17-20; 15:22 KJV).
-   Neglecting so great salvation (Hebrews 2:2,3 KJV).
-   Despising the plan of salvation (Hebrews 10:28,2 KJV 9).
-   Refusing Him that speaketh (Hebrews 12:25 KJV).
-   Refusing to come to Jesus (John 5:40 KJV).

3. Show the consequences of Sin (Romans 6:23; Revelation 21:8 KJV).
-   If he says he has not sinned (use I John 1:10 KJV).
-   If he says he has not sinned much (use James 2:10 KJV).
-   Emphasize the sin of unbelief (John 16:8,9; Hebrews 11:6 KJV).

4. Gladly share the beauty of the love of God and the gift of God. Carefully show the sinner John 3:16 and Isaiah 53:4-6. Why should God have gone to such extremes in providing such a wonderful salvation? How can anyone be indifferent in view of the suffering and agony of Jesus Christ in their place? (John 4:10; Romans 6:23 NIV).

5. Appeal to the element of hope.
    -   The hope of heaven (Matthew 19:21 NIV).

Dr. John Thomas Wylie

- The forgiveness of sins (Acts 10:42 NIV).
- Peace with God (Isaiah 36:3; 57:20,21 John 14:27 NIV).
- Fellowship with God (I John 1:3 NIV).

6. Appeal to his desire to be a blessing to others. Read to him what Jesus prayed in John 17:19. In saving others (Daniel 12:3; James 5:20 NIV).

3. The Procrastinator.
    1. Examples. There are those of the world who state, "How about we sit tight until tomorrow to choose for Jesus Christ." Many occasions the sun hasn't appeared on the morrow. Some state that they will contemplate eternity later on, and need to have their indulgence now. It's anything but difficult to put off a decision with respect to salvation, however we should work while it is yet day for the night cometh when no man can work" (John 9:4). We are still in the "longsuffering" days (II Peter 3:9). Focuses and Counterpoint:
        - "I'll hold up until I am more established." (II Samuel 19:35; Ecclesiastes 1'2:1-2; Hebrews 3:13; Proverbs 29:1 NIV.
        - "I would prefer not to do it this evening." (Proverbs 1:24-31 NIV).
        - "I'll need to thin about it."
        - "Hold up until I begin in business." (Matthew 6:33; Luke 12:16-21); James 4:13-17 NIV).

2. God's answers are an effective response to procrastinators.
   - "Today is the day of salvation" (II Corinthians NIV 6:2).
   - "Boast not thyself of tomorrow" (Proverbs 24:1 NIV. The sinner can't pick his own time (Genesis 6:3; John 6:44 NIV).
   - Seek ye the Lord while He may be found" (Isaiah 55:6 NIV).
   - "In what manner will we escape if we neglect so great salvation" (Hebrews 2:3 NIV).
   - "Seek ye first the kingdom of God" (Matthew 6:33 NIV).

3. Importance of a prompt decision. The thief on the cross, the Philippian jailor, Zaccheus, the Publican, were saved that day they were drawn nearer with the subject of salvation. Theirs was not a development into salvation or into interminable life, yet they were saved when they accepted. Responsibility ought to be set on early decisions for Jesus Christ.
   The obligation of parents in leading their youngsters to Christ at an early age is great. Once a child is in his adolescents, and particularly when he is past his teens, there is significantly less probability of his being saved.

4. Deathbed Conversions. Some state, "I'll hold up until my death, and at that point acknowledge Christ." They point to the apologetic hoodlum on the cross. However, just a single thief repented; the other was lost. An individual who supposes he can acknowledge Christ in his eleventh hour may die at

Dr. John Thomas Wylie

10:30. Procrastination is unsafe,dangerous and might be forever deadly.

4. The Sinner Who Says: "I Have Sinned Too Greatly."
    1. Jesus Christ came to save sinners - lost men, not good men., (Luke 5:31,32; 19:10; I Timothy 1:15 NIV).
        - Paul was chief of sinners. Jesus Christ saved him (I Timothy 1:15 KJV).
        - Your transgressions are as scarlet? (Isaiah 1:18 KJV).
        - You are lost? (Luke 19:10NIV).
        - David was a killer (murderer) and a sinner. He confessed and was forgiven. (Psalm 32:5 NIV).
        - Jesus won't cast anybody out. (John 6:37). (See likewise Isaiah 40:2; 43:25; 44:22; 53:4,5,6; 55:7; Matthew 9:12,13; Hebrews 7:25; I John 1:9 NIV).
        - Whosoever will may come" signifies anybody without regard to the sort of sin. (John 3:16; Romans 10:13; Revelation 22:1 NIV7).

    2. Some think it is past the point of no return - they have sinned away the day of grace.
        - Jesus won't cast out anybody (John 6:37 NIV.) He isn't willing that any should (perish) die (II Peter 3:9 NIV). Today is as still the day of salvation (II Corinthians 6:2 NIV).
        - The inconvenience for the most part is that the sinner won't come. (John 5:40; 7:17 KJV).

    3. Some think they have submitted the inexcusable (unpardonable) sin.
        - The individual who is concerned about having submitted this sin can rest assured he has not

committed it. The way that he is concerned is proof that the Holy Spirit is as yet endeavoring with him. Satan frequently uses such verses as Matthew 12:31,32; Hebrews 6:4-6; 10:26,27; I John 5:16 KJV to discourage the individuals who wish to be saved.

- However, a period comes when the Spirit, opposed and offended (resisted and insulted), stops endeavoring. At that point the sinner's case becomes hopeless. (Genesis 6:3; Proverbs 1:24-31; 29:1; Hosea 4:17; Acts 7:51 KJV.

- There is no content in the Bible which obstructs any individual who needs salvation or restoration.

4. Some state they should move toward becoming better. The sinner can't improve himself. (Jeremiah 2:22; 13:23; James 2:10).
    Memory Verses: Proverbs 28:13; 29:1; Romans 14:23; Hebrews 2:2,3; James 4:17; I John 5:17; Revelation 21:8 KJV.

Study Questions

How Did You Rate?

1. "Almost thou persuadest me to be a Christian" was spoken by which of the following procrastinators:
    _____Thief On The Cross _____Agrippa; _____Festus;
    _____Pilate

2. What answers could be given to the following types of procrastinators:
    _____ "I'll have to wait until I am better."
    _____ "I'll wait until I am older."

3. How would you reply to the procrastinator who says:
    -   "I'll have my fun first.'
    -   "I'll have to think more about it."

4. Suggest a procedure for dealing with the self satisfied.

5. What are the usual answers of the self-righteous?

6. What is the only righteousness acceptable to God? How can a sinner obtain it?

7. Suggest a method for dealing with the indifferent and unconcerned.

What Do You Think - Yes or No?

- A self-satisfied unbeliever more often than not has his very own religion of acts of kindness which he accepts will be adequate to God.
- Sickness, difficulty, or a passing in the family are regularly a surprisingly beneficial development as they cause an unconcerned individual to understand his need of salvation.
- The issue with the unconcerned is numbness.
- numbness with respect to his risky spiritual condition.
- Abel is a case of a man whose acts of kindness as a means for salvation were objected to God.
- If an individual can be saved by acts of kindness, Christ died in vain.
- God requests righteousness, perfection so as to get to paradise. subsequently, salvation is conceivable just through an perfect substitute, Jesus Christ.
- Before the cross people were saved by keeping the Law; notwithstanding, since the cross, salvation is by faith in Jesus Christ's sacrifice.
- Even a good man, for example, Nicodemus, was considered by God as a lost sinner, with a hopelessly insidious heart.
- The way that an individual is intrigued and worried in being spared is a good sign that he has not committed the indefensible, unpardonable sin.
- David, who committed the transgressions (sins) of homicide and infidelity, proclaimed himself in Psalm 51 to be the "head of sinners."
- The huge sin in this age, which censures people, is unbelief.

Dr. John Thomas Wylie

An Invitation To The Unsaved…

Is it true that you are Ready To Receive God's Free Gift?

IN CASE THAT YOU will be, you have to approach him in petition. You may supplicate your own petition. Or on the other hand, in the event that you need assistance in praying, you may use coming up the sinner's prayer that you really make it your own confession.

> Lord Jesus,
>
> I realize I am a sinner and need your forgiveness. I know you died on the cross for me. I currently abandon my transgressions and request that you forgive me. I presently welcome you into my heart and life. I currently trust you as my Savior and follow you as Lord.
>
> Thanks to You for saving me. Amen.

Did you solicit Jesus to forgive you from your transgressions (sins)?

Did you request that he save you?

Did you give Jesus unlimited oversight (absolute control) of your life?

Provided that this is true, welcome to God's family!

Why not take a brief reprieve and express gratitude toward Him for saving you.

What Does Jesus Want
You To Do Now?

TO START WITH, HE needs you to have confirmation (assurance) of your salvation. You can be sure you have eternal life:

1. Since you have been born again and birth is a one-time experience (See II Corinthians 5:17 NIV).

2. On account of your commitment. You did what the Bible instructed you to do (See Romans 10:13 KJV).

3. As a result of God's witness (see John 5:24 KJV).

4. Due to God's promise (See John 5:24 KJV).

5. Second, as proof of giving Jesus control of your life, he needs you to openly admit him and follow him in baptism and church enrollment.

    The Bible says, "Those who had received his word were baptized; and ... the Lord was adding to their number day by day the those who were being saved" (Acts 2:41-47 KJV).

    Third, Jesus needs you to develop into a strong, dependable follower. The Bible says, "Like newborn babes, long for the pure milk of the word, that by it you grow in respect to salvation (I Peter 2:2,3 KJV).

Dr. John Thomas Wylie

There are four absolutes in Growth:

1. Food. Spiritual nourishment is God's Word (the Bible). You should peruse it, think about it, retain it, practice it, and hear it taught and preached.

2. Breathing. Spiritual breathing is supplication (prayer). Spend time consistently conversing with God about all that you do; about your needs and issues; about family and companions; and reveal to Him how much you love Him and how appreciative you are.

3. Exercise. Spiritual exercise implies helping other people, seeing, giving time and vitality to God's work, and being a living testimony to the world you live in.

4. Rest. Spiritual rest implies worship: both public and private worship. Rest implies being still and waiting on God. It implies physical and spiritual renewal.

    Fourth. Jesus need you to encounter triumph over transgression (sin) in your day by day life. The Bible says, "For whatever is born of God overcome the world; and this is the victory that has overcome the world - our faith" (I John 5:4).

    1. The Christian life is difficult, but victory is assured because "Greater is He who is in you, than he who is in the world" (I John 4:4 KJV).

    2. Indeed, even with victory assured, there will be acts of disobedience and disappointments due to your human nature. In any case, God has given a means by which you can be washed down (cleansed) of every day sins. His Word says, "If we confess our sins, He is faithful

and righteous to forgive us our sins and to cleanse us from all unrighteousness" (I John 1:9).

3. Even with victory assured, when you sin, don't deny it or excuse it. Rather, name your transgression (sin) to God, and claim His promise of forgiveness.

Bibliography

Coleman, R. E. (1987) The Master Plan Of Evangelism.
Grand Rapids, MI.: Fleming H. Revell, A Division Of
Baker Book House

Hadidian, A. (1979) Successful Discipling. Chicago, Ill.:
Moody Press

The Holy Bible (1964) Authorized King James Version.
Chicago, Ill.: J. G. Ferguson

The Holy Bible (1982) New Interpreter's Version. Grand
Rapids, MI.: Thomas Nelson Inc. (Used By Permission)

The Holy Bible (1953) The Revised Standard Version.
Nashville, TN.: Thomas Nelson & Sons (Used By
Permission)

The New Testament In The Language of The People (1937,
1949) Chicago, Ill.: Charles B Williams, Bruce Humphries,
Inc. Moody Bible Institute (Used By Permission)

About The Author

THE REVEREND DR. JOHN Thomas Wylie is one who has dedicated his life to the work of God's Service, the service of others; and being a powerful witness for the Gospel of Our Lord and Savior Jesus Christ. Dr. Wylie was called into the Gospel Ministry June 1979, whereby in that same year he entered The American Baptist College of the American Baptist Theological Seminary, Nashville, Tennessee.

As a young Seminarian, he read every book available to him that would help him better his understanding of God as well as God's plan of Salvation and the Christian Faith. He made a commitment as a promising student that he would inspire others as God inspires him. He understood early in his ministry that we live in times where people question not only who God is; but whether miracles are real, whether or not man can make a change, and who the enemy is or if the enemy truly exists.

Dr. Wylie carried out his commitment to God, which has been one of excellence which led to his earning his Bachelors of Arts in Bible/Theology/Pastoral Studies. Faithful and obedient to the call of God, he continued to matriculate in his studies earning his Masters of Ministry from Emmanuel Bible College, Nashville, Tennessee & Emmanuel Bible College, Rossville, Georgia. Still, inspired to please the Lord and do that which is well – pleasing in the Lord's sight, Dr. Wylie recently on March 2006, completed his Masters of Education degree with a concentration in Instructional Technology earned at The American Intercontinental University, Holloman Estates, Illinois. Dr. Wylie also previous to this, earned his Education

Specialist Degree from Jones International University, Centennial, Colorado and his Doctorate of Theology from The Holy Trinity College and Seminary, St. Petersburg, Florida.

Dr. Wylie has served in the capacity of pastor at two congregations in Middle Tennessee and Southern Tennessee, as well as served as an Evangelistic Preacher, Teacher, Chaplain, Christian Educator, and finally a published author, writer of many great inspirational Christian Publications such as his first publication:

"Only One God: Who Is He?" – published August 2002 via formally 1ˢᵗ books library (which is now AuthorHouse Book Publishers located in Bloomington, Indiana & Milton Keynes, United Kingdom) which caught the attention of **The Atlanta Journal Constitution Newspaper.**

Dr. Wylie is happily married to Angel G. Wylie, a retired Dekalb Elementary School teacher who loves to work with the very young children and who always encourages her husband to move forward in the Name of Jesus Christ. They have Four children, 11 grand-children and one great-grandson all of whom they are very proud. Both Dr. Wylie and Angela Wylie serve as members of the Salem Baptist Church, located in Lilburn, Georgia, where the Reverend Dr. Richard B. Haynes is Senior pastor.

Dr. Wylie has stated of his wife: "she knows the charm and beauty of sincerity, goodness, and purity through Jesus Christ. Yes, she is a Christian and realizes the true meaning of loveliness as the reflection as her life of holy living gives new meaning, hope, and purpose to that of her husband, her children, others may say of her, "Behold the handmaiden of the Lord." A Servant of Jesus Christ!

About The Book

ONE NEEDS TO GO to the New Testament, and the Gospels specifically, to truly observe the evangelistic plan of Jesus. They after all are the main eye-witness accounts that we have of the Savior, Jesus at work. (Luke 1:2,3; John 20:30; 21:24; I John 1:1 NIV).

Certainly, the Gospels were composed fundamentally to indicate us Jesus Christ, the Son of God, and that by faith we can have life in his name (John 20:31). Be that as it may, what once in a while we neglect to acknowledge is that the revelation of that life in Christ incorporates the manner in which he lived and trained others so to live. We should remember that the witnesses who composed the books not just witnessed the truth; they were changed by it.

The task of this publication, "The Believer's Guide To Personal Evangelism," is to bring people to faith in Jesus Christ, an individual should unmistakably and coherently present the need for Jesus Christ, and the provision God has made to address that issue. While there are numerous approaches, this publication puts forward the plain facts, and the directness of the straightforwardness (simplicity) of the gospel Our Lord And Saviour, Jesus Christ.

Reverend Dr. John Thomas Wylie

Printed in the United States
By Bookmasters